UNITED STATES

UNITED STATES

DAN FEATHERSTON

FACTORY SCHOOL
2005

United States by Dan Featherston

First Edition, Factory School 2005

Heretical Texts: Volume 1, Number 1
Series Editor: Bill Marsh

ISBN 1-60001-040-7

Thanks to the editors of the following publications, where some of these poems first appeared: *26, A.BACUS, Aufgabe, Can We Have Our Ball Back, Cultural Society, First Intensity, House Organ, Kiosk, Milk, New American Writing, Poetry New York, Quarry Press Broadside Series, Range, Sulfur, University of Arizona Poetry Center Broadside Series, & Ur Vox.* "Clown" appeared in the anthology *A Phylum Press Selection: Little Critic No 17*, ed. Richard Deming & Nancy Kuhl (Ballybeg, Ireland: Coracle Press, 2003); *United States* appeared in the Phylum Press chapbook series.

Cover art: Octavia Davis, Bill Marsh
Production Assistants: Octavia Davis, J.R. Osborn

FACTORY SCHOOL
factoryschool.org

For Rachel–
beauty & grace

Contents

WORLD NEWS

Aerial Photograph of an Elephant Graveyard

after Peter Beard

under the airplane shadow
savannah grass worn in a circle
one dead elephant   in the center
where it fell   circling the other
the shape of sorrow a circle
cut into the earth   turning round
the other   as if it could somehow
return somehow turn its own sorrow
back into the earth

In Gericault's *Raft of the Medusa*

I recognize what wave regards:
shirt sleeves & sail fleck,
wave regarding wave in mutual blindness
over horizon lines of floating news,
hallucinated harbors
                              what a man signals
regarded as gull wing, cloud wisp, white cap,
stuffing the hole in the sky where men drown
daily, drawn down through the appearances.

But the raft is real–
                              mote in the wide wreck
we call earth, divining counter-force
in limb & timber, taut rigging
& foreshortened gesture,
propped head & sail meditating direction:
who isn't rafted to human?
who isn't shipwrecked in mortal,
marooned equidistant from horizons–
whatever we look toward,
waving under a bright & empty sky.

Oaxacan Masks

1.

The face in the landscape & the landscape in the face
drift in mutual exile.

We do not know which way the mask faces,
whether *way* turns outward
or tumbles in.

Eden is Any-Face, any
one who looks like you.

Looks-like-you dozes at the outpost of other.
Then lizards scuttle in,
spiders slip past the eyes.

Death is the vanishing point of resemblance.
There is horror in resemblance–
autonomy of *mere coincidence.*

He who called language self
called the book a face
held up to mind's transparency.

Where mind shines through–
fiction, death rehearsals.

2.

The mask-maker hollows holes
faces fill, tumid with outward,
heaped with prehistoric excrement:
reptiles, frog's amphibian–
both-sided, doubled, dubious
nature before bone & teeth
turned mask inward,
turning out over the landscape–
vestigial faces of fear
impacted in molar, skeleton, brain case.

All around the mask-maker
wood curls to floor's
nevermore, turning face
inside out, turning fear
inside out.

The mask is a limit to the face falling inward.
The mask is a limit to the face falling outward.
For example, God.

At the surface of a mask
instinct & extinct merge,
each face the tenuous profile
of survivannihilation.

3.

Outside the mask-maker's studio
a grasshopper squats
in the wood pile.

Its stillness is wood.
Its stillness is a face
surfacing through predatory air.

Horses

> *Dawn is the head of a sacrificed horse.*
> — Milton Kessler

1. Old World Horses

Horse hair snow wisp–
landscape's Flemish
pennant fray & blond wind

*

Tethered necks
bent
shapely to water

*

Rain bloated photograph
horses tangled in barbwire
dead in long ditches

2. New World Horses

Shrunk to chrome ornaments
Blurred billboard stampede
Raising batons above the riot
war above the horizon
Lengthening the stride of capitalism

*

A sloped earth saddled

Spurred horizon's
stirrup– little star

*

Ear to the ground, listening to America

Cavalry advancing
the rhythm of violence

*

Cowboy Buddha:

    Eye of my horse
    center of the floating world

*

Deus ex equus

    Conquistadors grown
    gold out of horseback

*

Western Tragedy:

    If noon arrives before the horse
    hang him from a tree

*

A man freezing to death
sees a house in his horse
huddled inside
the death that precedes him

A man freezing to death
sees a hearse in his horse
huddled inside
the death that resembles him

*

Head massive, epic

who will notice
the little eye
where something painful
contracts?

*

Black Elk's four-horse heaven
bound to the book of massacre,
bound to Revelation

*

Night *mara*

       Europe's incubus
folded into saddlebags
smuggled into America's
many million deaths

*

Night *mara*

       She who sits
upon a sleeping man's chest

he cannot breathe
waking to shake
a weight that lay upon him
       night mares
       asleep in Spanish galleons

Modern Times

for Charlie Chaplin

The Conveyances

How be attentive to this stream of bolts
while breasts, buttons, & fire hydrants
wrench loose in the attention?

The work is the tension, holding to one
thing repeated down the line.

But it's the belt that moves,
not these bodies
disappeared in the conveyances.

Anything tightened trembles.

Lunch

Hunger juts perpendicular to the machine;
it is this mouth we are obliged to feed,
the foreman who stands before
the machine, minding its intricacies.

But mind is not outside. It is noon
& the mind is a clock
telling time. But the telling
is within time. The head,
fed chicken, custard, coffee,
disappears into afternoon.

The Division of Labor

The machine is endlessly incomplete.
It is a mirror, mediating exchanges
between subject & object
where money would be eyes
shining behind the labor of division.

Oil

Through the hole in van Gogh's head
the landscape changes: starry turbines
merge with rivets & wheels.
The hole is the space
between any two coordinates–
spot weld where angels with oil
cans pirouette like cypress wicks,
burning between belabored
heaven & belabored earth.

Wealth

What flag is this, waving between
the back of a flatbed
& front of a worker's march?

Chance rounds the corner, rounds the false
four-square precision between
what I say & what I mean.

Or is this the same flag
waving at every intersection?
Do we mean to bring down the wood beam
over our own door,
                              wealth: this weight of roofs
& capital propped by the bent broom of improbable means?

There is a wealth of improbability.

There is wealth in probability–
tin can glint of cut crystal
while floorboards give way
under actual weight. Gives
way to this small meal between two,
candle's slushed light soldering wall to wall–
enough to live by, drill swiss from cheddar,
trace ice rinks from floorboards: love,
perhaps, this alchemy of poverty & wealth,
is & would be: the napkin hung in the drapery,
the grape vine & milking cow at every threshold.

The Department Store

Every story is a situation. Outside the departmentalized
mind, a man's whole life rises up in one building.

Several stories above you, she sleeps in satin & fur.
In morning your tugged shirt
tails uproot you from a dream–
some other story in which you fall asleep beneath her.

The Jail

The jail contains the traffic of associations,
vagrancies outside the law of appearances–
comic-tragic banter like tin cup
rattlings until the rock is rolled away:
the socialist gone into the city,
dreaming of fish & loaves,
rogues knitting escapes,
clues dispersed in the crowd
shoveled back behind bars–
the dross, the derelict,
the rum barrel run-off,
your critique of wealth
an eye wink the diameter of a bullet hole.

Dinner

The object of desire circulates over the dance.
The platter may be out-of-reach capital,
an allegory of the dance itself.

The platter will come late, sans entrée.
Because "main course" cannot be quantified,
you look for the roasted duck
under the butter dish.
Meanwhile, it hangs like crepe
draped from a chandelier
whose light is also part of the dance.

The History of Laughter

She would be these lines you take with you
onto the dance floor, recalling her to you,
glancing under the coat sleeves
of who-I-believe-myself-to-be.

But be is false. The lines will not hold.
Uncuffed, she flies from you.
The music stalls.

There are shadowy figures, bewildered at the periphery.
They say:

> We have come here tonight for news of modern times.
> We have seen, in the modern mass, a roasted duck
> become a football. We have seen you do an end run
> around what we believe ourselves to be. Let punchline
> be Eucharist, inverting expectation. Let it bolt from
> the blue, from the smoke stack top hat the impossible
> rabbit & dove, the lost key, the gentleman's glove . . .

> Let it come from nothing. Let humor be the perfect
> machine manufacturing useless objects. When we
> come to arrest you, leave a trail of scattered chairs. Let
> laughter ignite like history closing in behind you. Let
> be step ahead of its debris– these heartbreaks that keep
> the reel turning toward inevitable sunsets.

Clown

                    pockets turned out on thighs
studded with inside: exstrophic sleeves,
moebial holsters flanked to flaccid
crown pulled down to waist in wilted rays,
walking a compost of inverted images.

What's funny about *klutz*,
about clutter of clutched
muscle melted in hot laughter?
What's haha about loosed
like hula hoop,
                    spasm slipped
back, pedaling head over peel in puddled pants?

Over the ring we range to circumscribe,
spot spectacle in hot-white
rims of radio bands, newspapers . . .

over the ring   who bears the weight of human pyramid?
Whose shoes aren't too   on groundswells
of lumpy backs, bulldozed bones,
frailties we stand upon
walking the tightrope smirk,
                              register of the little
weight we are   wobbling in the rope's
grin that would drop us
                              deadpan.

Columbine

> *To be furious is to be frighted out of fear,*
> *And in that mood the dove will peck the estridge.*
> — Shakespeare

When will America recognize the face of ignorance
under the death mask of hatred?
When will America recognize the face of fear
under the face of ignorance
under the death mask of hatred?
When will America recognize the tragedy in farce,
grimace & raillery in *sannio*
mocking the principal characters
now Columbine is a school, war zone, flower, dovelike
sweet heart of Harlequin's stuffed shirt, Media's *buffo,*
the bloated trench coat forcemeat filler
answering for the dead:

> *Now in the skin of a goat, now in the skin of a tiger, variegated in color,*
> *now laced with shabby ribbons, sparse beard, sloe eyes,*
> *a black half-mask, wooden sword once the curved staff of Bacchus.*

*

The proposition: *There comes a time when only Anger is Love*
& hate answers hate in war's global combine,
two by two the turbine turning through Columbine
in love with Harlequin, "demon huntsman"
America will not face as its own:
he who would hunt his own,
whose eyes narrow with hate,
cowering before Father-War's poltroonery–
Uncle Sam Pantaloon propagating his own image,
in love with the hunter
who propagates what Harlequin loves–
sweet heart of Columbine
where Media stumbles over campus,
dumb to *campos* & factioning.

Media hears no strife in her daughter,
her dovelike Columbine
propagating the sweet heart of innocence;

will not hear how she gives birth to strife
in bed with Father-War, propagating the lie
in Columbine, farce of doves born free
from hunters, phallic choirs, the gun show.

*

Then Hate would counter-balance
Media's Doctrine of Humor–
high choler trench coat,
a fome of blood
doth turn up
in his head, who said:

> *I cannot wait to kill*
> *& I don't care if I live or die*

bunkered down in Littletown anonymity,
an arsenal of fear propagating counter-images,
& so kid gunman would shoot a hole
through himself in Columbine
whose fear reflects his own:

> *He was walking toward me.*
> *I saw a grenade in his hand.*

*

When only Anger is Love, Hate counters Media
who would hear no strife in columbine,
their necks colored soft as doves–
the comedic, void of tragedy,
the comedic void in tragedy propagating farce
that did arouse political suspicion.

Media notes how *Harlequin had over his left eye*
a wart which covered half his cheek,
& for this reason assumed the trench coat
that hangs, now, at both ends of a century
entrenched in war, where Columbine
would rise up from the trench
coat thrown over Media
thrown over into darkness
> *whose hands & head are of wood, the body a cloth pocket,*

Father-War *working the arms, moving the head,*
hand thrust into the hollow neck,
& Media, duped by Harlequin's mask:

> *But the children– they are columbine,*
> *They are lamb of my land!*

*

There is no innocence, no wall of wood crosses
& stuffed animals plugging holes
in Harlequin where Media's wooden head
fuels strife & division– trench coats divining signs,
dividing monstrous from human.

Take, instead, trench coat set against shoulder pads,
farce stuffing the loaded jersey of fear
puffed up in division, the home field
advantage in numbered jerseys
who stand counted in *campos*
against Harlequin's *rabbit tail,*
fox tail, rabbit ears of ridicule–
farce upon farce, & all is *campos,*
                    even our high schools unsafe
laboratories of hatred.

*

In Columbine's sweet heart the parti-colored
confusion of Harlequin in Media's eyes,
Media in Harlequin's eyes,
Mafia, *mi familia* that propagates no one,
gunning down the halls in laughter,
in Media's farce:
          They were only children!
fed into Moloch who is, now,
children cannibalizing children,
children putting on trench coats
sewn in Father-War's factories:
Dauchau, Hiroshima, high schools
balkanized, mimicking Media's
mass confusion, mimicking
Pantaloon's propagation,
who say of their children

But they are columbine!
& turn away in the love-hate turbine.

*

Now Father-War in Congress cries:
       It is images unholy!
       Tear down the images!
       Tear down false idols of fiction!
       Take the diary out of the basketball
       dribbling in the court of virtual strife!
       Pull down first-person shooters!
       Take Manson out of our Marilyn,
       our sweet Columbine
       hunted by Harlequin mask!

*

What is the face behind Harlequin's mask?
       Mercurial, of ignorance, naivete,
       stupidity; of violent movements
       & outrageous blackguardisms,
       at once insolent, mocking, clownish,
       &, above all, obscene,
what Media & Congress would not see,
tearing down the mask,
leaving NATO airstrikes intact,
the "terrible mistake" of laser-guided
civilian casualties; would tear down the idols
& leave Yugoslav henchmen intact,
carving, with broken glass, the Serbian
cross into a Kosovar woman's back.

*

Media worships no idols but her own–
idols of innocence & ignorance
where Harlequin bunkers down
under Littletown trench coats,
Columbine's How-Happen-Here?
when here, now, is everywhere;
therefore, nowhere: Media's
nowhere farce of monstrous
trench coats & columbine innocence.

-26-

They mimic the maker, mimic Media & Pantaloon—
sanniones stumbling over the banana peel
of 111,000,000 dead, 20th century, by war.

Duncan:

> *Reject Hitler as the enemy*
> *and you have to go to battle*
> *against the very nature of Man,*
> *against the truth of things.*
> *Hitler cannot be defeated;*
> *he must be acknowledged and understood.*

Harlequin, rejected by the marines,
unfit to mimic Father-War,
walks out into the world
war in Columbine.

> *I heard explosions.*
> *I thought it was a prank,*
> *a person outside columbine*

the farce,
the confusion.

Brothers Quay

1.

Maze of alleys, mirrors, dimly lit shop windows.
An oversized head's craft of ravaged plaster.
Eye's liquid wobble, dandelion clock brain.
Ice cube's frame-by-frame to say a window
stuffed with steel wool, ping pong balls.
Anamorphic reindeer.
Bullet fixed in one testicle.
Really all this sublime belief no one's complicity
in furtive glances & choreographed shadows
shifting a palimpsest of music, literature, dance
& architecture– impossible spaces,
secret relationships of spastic machinery,
occluded mirrors, fetish dust, feverish dreams.
The cryptic, the lyrical, & the metaphysical
(not to mention modern impotence, epiphany,
paranoia & despair) all in tiny, mechanical spasms,
as if a mind were two voices, puppeted,
enmeshed in hermetic interiors.

2.

A solitary figure gazes out his window– somnambular
wanderings in the baroque watchmaker's mausoleum,
generatio aequivoca of undead slumber, crumbling
pentimento. We ask our machines to act as much,
if not more–open to vast uncertainties, mistakes,
disorientations–in order to trap fugitive encounters.
Pitted, deformed head perched on a tangle of wire.
Malicious eye's fixed stare. A single hair
protruding out of a soft mole. Wire homunculus:
seduction or disconnected interior monologues.
Jittery macro lens of depthless field out of staggered
camera's fast pan flicker focus melange of ladders,
landscapes, painted backgrounds–
credible arrangements all rootless & abandoned,
tweaked out of crumbling fabric,
privacies in the lives of slumbering materials.

3.

Floppy puppet's burlesque death mask & porcelain
doll head serial numbered like concentration
trapped in sawdust & cloth's sinister dream compound–
zone of secret liberties fermenting in conspiratorial climates.
Out of cold war phantoms & fossilized hierarchies,
we disappear into any country.

Imperial Antidote

If it harms you
beat it against
what it is not.

If it harms you
throw it against
what it is not.

If it harms you
bury it so deep
it resembles
nothing.

Evidence

Dear Sir:

Those trial records *it was common to shoot people on bridges so the bodies would fall into the river* along with other documentation *& float down the current* were destroyed in a fire *or hide them in clandestine graves or mineshafts* caused by a terrorist attack on army installations *or dump them in rivers or in the ocean* where part of the documentation *or dynamite them* was located.

Camouflage

The invisible prey upon the visible.

It was in nature to deceive
in her nature to conceive
a bright toy
a canister of sunlight
exploded in her hands.

The invisible prey upon the visible.

It was in nature to deceive
in his nature to conceive
a play of dappled leaves
in sniper fatigues
gunning down civilians in daylight.

The invisible prey upon the visible.

Because of its success in the field
we will continue using
cluster bomb canisters
skidding gold under
fire bombed cars,
rubbled walls–
wherever life's hidden
her face under gauze
too close too deep to remove
the invisible seeps through
as trauma: *an unnatural fear of bright colors,*
afraid to touch under life's
beauty & bright surprise
death surfaces behind her eyes.

Pied Beauty

after Gerard Manley Hopkins

Glory be to God for shrapneled things–
  For skies of couple-color and the burning towns;
   For bullet-holes in stipple upon men who run;
Fresh-firestrafe cluster-falls; fighter wings;
  Landscape plotted and pierced– rape, raze, and pillage;
   And all tanks, their gear and travel and whim.

Counter all things Arab, Muslim, strange;
  Whatever is ethnic, other (who knows why?)
   With swift blow; sweep scour; bedraggled grim;
He fathers-forth nothing whose life is past change:
          Kill him.

Kosovar Child's Still Life with Agitprop

Here are crayons & paper to gather intelligence,
what won't reconnoiter exact colors & shapes,
for example aerial photographs
that may or may not be
for example civilian casualties
that may or may not be

We cannot explain why ethnic needs cleansing.
We cannot explain why the village was burned.
We cannot explain why your father dug a hole
then lay at the bottom with a bullet in his head.
We cannot explain why your mother was raped
then stabbed repeatedly in the face & chest.

Red: This is my mother & father.
We cannot say whether the map was misread.
Orange: This is my house burning.
We cannot say whether Serbian or NATO fire.
Green: This is a tank & this is a soldier.
We cannot say whether tractor or armored personnel carrier.

We cannot say for certain circles
jerk between fact & fiction
for example 4,000 ethnic Albanians
walking in a circle from Kosovo
to Macedonia to Albania
to Monte Negro to Kosovo.

We cannot say why the pattern retraces
pushed out of a crayon
pushing & pushing
into paper: this & this & this.

Sentences

Sentences pass between capital boundaries,
each dome's plunge upward an allegory
of providence. In the province of allegory
the horizon is crime manufacturing laws.

*

There is a one-way mirror between the sentence
& its execution. Because the executioner
has no face, the sentence is impersonal,
handed down through the state:
the set of circumstances or attributes
we intuit but cannot perceive.

*

When the clock hands fold together
the switch lifts
the body jolts.

The sentence reappears in newspaper minutiae:
The lights in the town flickered.
Someone's bathroom mirror dimmed.
A glass of milk turned gray.

The clock & the sun & the holy volt
Amen.

*

Seven marksmen.
One of the rifles
contains a blank.
No one knows
what is being fired.
We fire.
The blank ends the sentence.

*

In the public square, the crime hangs down through time.
The body was a way to perceive the crime.

It was not about death.
There was no broken neck.
There was not even a neck
& the rope was tied to itself.

*

Hate is a weight handled, picked up off the ground.
Taking aim, he throws through a hole in himself where she kneels.

The men were the first to throw stones.
They called it just: *Just this old law
handed to us from the ground up;
a sentence meaning itself.*

At noon a mound of stones covers her.
They say it is natural that she has gone back into the earth.

He feels clean, coming away from the stones,
As if my own filth were lifted from me.

*

When his heart grew heavy, he would throw things from himself. He threw words & balls & bottles, but the weight was still there. He threw shoes & mirrors & lamps, but the weight was still there. He threw statues & horses & houses, but the weight was still there.

A woman came to him & asked, "What are you doing?" "I am trying to throw off this weight, but it is too heavy." "Throw the world itself from you," she said. "Then you will understand."

He threw the world from himself & drifted upward like a stone. He looked down & saw there was nothing. He looked up & saw there was nothing. He looked to the left & to the right & saw there was nothing. Nothing but the weight.

Bodies from Rwanda

10,000 corpses pipeline into Lake Victoria, Uganda,
where Ngoga Murumba, loading bodies into trucks
for mass graves, pulls from lakewater hyacinth
five drowned children roped to their mother's corpse:

one tied to her left leg
one tied to her right leg
one tied to her left arm
one tied to her right arm
one tied to her back

*

*The victim was lowered into a stream or pond by men holding
ropes, one on each bank. If the body floated, witchcraft was
proved, on the theory that water rejected a witch. If the body
sank, the accused was innocent, although frequently dead of
drowning. The decision was largely dependent upon the men
who held the ropes.*

*

Downshore, Ugandan fishermen, sewing holes into their nets,
turn their oars shoreward. Where there is no direction,
no oar to turn against the water,
Murumba feels only numb,
mind palled in sheer mass of attention to the net.

*

Downshore, a Ugandan boy, drinking lakewater,
tastes his own skin floating in his palms,
tastes his own death
slipping between his fingers.

*

Extra locum torturae

Let the body be the instrument of its own torture.
Soli Deo Gloria. No blame.

As for the Rwandan woman who gave life from life,
let life be the instrument of its own torture.
Soli Deo Gloria. No blame.

Threat Conditions

after Arthur Rimbaud

Green, Blue, Yellow, Orange, Red: Threat Conditions,
One day I will tell your latent fear:
Green, low risk of refined exercises
Preplanned around protective measures,

Vulnerabilities; Blue of guarded condition,
Checking, reviewing, updating;
Yellow elevated, increasing surveillance
In assessing further refinement;

Orange, high risk, coordination of armed forces;
Preparing to work at an alternate site
Or with a dispersed world force;

Red, severe Risk of emergency response,
Closing facilities; constraining;
–Redirecting personnel to critical needs!

CIA Lexicon

Imam, which way is don't move east?
Which way is open road west?
Imam, we are hand grenade brothers.
We are socks, hat, coat.
We are machine pants.
Where I put down gun, Imam,
we are stand up brothers.

Which way is water? Where is bread?
Where we are, brothers, I am here,
which is where I am.

Don't move ammunition overcoat.
Don't move hand knife stand up.
Don't move water bread sit down.
Brothers, don't move.
We are where we are.

Imam, we are bread. We are brothers.
We are pistol sit down stand up hand grenade.
We are bicycle knife overcoat brothers.
We are, Imam, east west open road brothers.
Are we?

UNITED STATES

The United States themselves are essentially the greatest poem.
								– Walt Whitman

What / if lilacs last in *this* dooryard bloomd?
								– Robert Duncan

1.

Trash can
fire fuels
a ring of hands

2.

Hanged man
dangled down
through high
blue quietude
& noon

3.

Hibiscus flowers
shrivel inward
a hardball blue
fist of sunlight's
final folding fact

4.

Conquistador's *vanilla*

Shapely little sheaths
Our Lady of the Trees

5.

Elephant pyramid

wobbles on a ball
& acrobats
imagine that
all's laughter after the fall

6.

Day
light
bulb

Rain
falling in the occan

7.

River raised one
drop the junked
car sunk under

8.

Hammer whack
fact of wood

A boundary is everything else

9.

Paper leaves shook
the book of trees

10.

Plates clatter
stacked flat
     a useful emptiness

11.

Not air not
things steeped there

Place takes place

12.

You stand behind
your voice
an afterthought

13.

Hummingbird's blurred
slenderness
centered
deep in the flower's sweet

14.

       Kore's honeyed language

Bees born of cattle's
tawny grammar
stammer in the trees

15.

Sediment
Sentiment

Rein in the heart

16.

Body
minds
convexity

17.

Depression begs
the question
pressed
under what

18.

Wall

profile of a room

19.

Nudged bricks
babble down
Puppets
puddle under string

Every thing
depends

20.

Bud Powell's asylum
key in the wall's
listen to this

21.

blooms
brief
given
grief

22.

Rain machine

A falling weight detonates
slowed to gutter
  stutters
    ground down
then shallows swift
& speed to puddle
  lustrous
under a force withdrawn

23.

       Photograph of a Hiroshima watch

What time it was
what time it is
when skin is
vapor
       & human
       a shadow past
       the blast's
       oblivion o'clock

24.

       Pentagon riddle

How many Nazis did it take
to screw a US flag
into the moon?

25.

       Moon walk

Red white blue flag
flutters falsely free

Exorbitant cold war tree

26.

       One small step

"The moon! The moon! The moon!"

The final frontier is pointing

27.

Pornography

As if surface could transform suffering

Sexual root of religion:
transubstantiation = orgasm

28.

Absent objects

Sadness of empty
chairs not being
there
		my you
		your where

Once talking across
the house now
carried out–
all that matter
as if all that
matters now
between us

There is a bird sings only at night
we never learned
the name
& tore each other apart
not listening

29.

Hands

ask what the mind
cannot give
take what the mind
cannot live

30.

Infinite Justice

infinite
just this

just this
grist of
bees
gist of
flag
manifold

31.

Legalese tautology

material
evidence

32.

In the Ptolemaic kitchen

we breathe through
our eyes cry
over the cut
onion's beauty of concentric worlds

33.

Conspiracy theory of wind

Each nation unconsciously acts out the secret drama of its flag

34.

Intelligence failure

Human bombs strapped with explosives
Shoe bombs
Shoeshine bombs
Music box & windup bombs
Bombs sitting in buses, walking into plazas,
eating pizzas, piloting bombs
disguised as planes disguised as
point A to point
being the failure of intelligence
is the failure of imagination
& the failure of imagination
the failure of empathy

35.

All laws translations
of an original crime
no one saw to speak

36.

How close is death to the surface of life?

As if nowhere were
somewhere else

37.

Because murder is a dead language
no one understands the crime
The last surviving speaker is dead
Those who heard it
can't recall what was said
They plead insanity
or say they were someone else

Every sentence is a translation

38.

This, too, will drown you

Narcissism that sees
only otherness

39.

Returning to a face
not memory
but a place

40.

This click click sick blue pixel flicker's
filler for
            Who are you?

41.

        Desert Storm

as if war were weather
& violence
a mirage of blood
vanished under radar

42.

        Enduring Freedom

as if
& as
we can

43.

When a rat chews off a corpse's nose
it is not about pain

Resemblance is hunger's refrain

44.

Skeleton key opens
every body
a door

45.

       Peacock the fabled poison-eater

Death's bright
beauty, then,
hides the hen

46.

Children stone what moves
divided by water they
do not understand
between movement
& their hands
holding stones–
violence born before
their own belated births,
& so throw stones
opposite water & birds

What is it wants apprehension
of all the departed
      the already born & moving away
so much to say
Don't leave me
      Don't leave me
or I will kill you

47.

Cicada sings what the sirens sing–
each death is a strident thing

Ears stoppered
sailing straight
through strait's
swift steering
away all the same

Each death is a little valve

48.

      World's Fair ruins

Stone steps lead down into water
such passages swans abide,
gliding out of place in the old world's
fair to say paired, a single life there,
wondering, now, those steps–
where they led

                  out of the head,
out of the heady romance of a gone
world's fair to say steps go into
nowhere love of ruins
like a shore's amplified closures

49.

      Star gazing

How little we
are no not
little but far
from close

How big we
are to say,
so far away,
there– that star
close as
who we are

50.

The bright step of a god withdrawn–

footstep worlds walk into being
       where the foot lifts
shaped to the maker's withdrawal

God is first artifact

DEMOCRACIES OF PERCEPTION

Catastrophe

tiny catgut exhaust a glitter sky without sea twisting
birds visible off shelves funny to say sequence of time a
kind of grammar a motion or a measure alarmed at the
pure pleasure plumes of radiation rosy fingered bombs
the blue pond in her shoulder a crucifix pinned to sky
screw twisting through rock leading back to itself shut
off from god blossoms deeply inside her hand that
thing in the dirt jerked green sprays fill a suddenness
deeply inside her body god scattered propellers inside
no tortoise green catastrophe gold juju & spoons
sucked straw bridge flock into flag sky & god glitter
moon curve funny prayer knot car lot pennant end over
end sings rickety river wind accordion braces troll nets
resembling a child's drawing the window to say catholic
hell without light resembling trilobite twisting through
rock shut off from god deeply inside that thing in the
dirt braces to fill catastrophe view of birds flickering
flag pointing green curve & glitter suddenness shelves

Man Asleep in Cardboard Box

cluster of permutations as pleasure exceeding a vessel
easily emptied bent to sorrow as if the body could
enter its own image as habit's smooth rut shaped by
explaining sky blue brickwork birds & trees move
brackish through man asleep in cardboard box driven
by death as guilt of origin twist of incident exceeding
a vessel bent to mean exceeding as between pleasures
the folded spread easily industry's weights & a mirror
in a house is patience to find one's place as passing
death's face arrives empty trees move through a foreign
body we no longer think asleep in cardboard to have a
house or hand in it this twist of incident's disorder bent
to sorrow

Anything Within Itself Seeks Round Shape

behind beauty's counter force of terror out there putting things inside each other also plums & kiwis the element of hysteria's every other commodity now a mirror of mind anyway if you need anything or whatever p.s. the map over the sink is ornament between man & the history of glass let's have breakfast putting things inside each other including within itself counter-hegemonic forces out there how you do art to capture or divide frozen peaches drizzled lemon juice brown sugar anything with some freedom behind beauty's counter force of terror out there exchanged for silk let's take two commodities & 10 yards of linen in the realm of discursive convention's declaratives including within itself or whatever p.s. children raised by animals what do they draw inside terror a big container also plums kiwis phoenician wheat in the realm of discursive let's have breakfast drizzled peach brown sugar no central vanishing point including within itself counter force seeks a mirror of mind always imminent to distribute transgressive dimensions in the realm of things behind beauty if you need to leave something out there raised by animals inside terror a big container as anything within itself seeks round shape

Despair

prayer bundle snake huddled in eden lifts old animal
despair itself a steppe of twilight small forsaken space
in slack images piled to delight those beaten extremes
even tears & people began to consume grass & moss
old shoes liquefied medley of animal despair piled to
delight those extremes even to consume in eden old
shoes whitewash bodies bad rulers a civil discord of
two worlds wholly liquefied in eternity what we have
forsaken to consume old animal despair no boundaries
lifting & what we have forsaken even tears & despair &
worlds contracted in eden like oil lifts then tears of old
animal despair & people began to consume grass moss
old shoes whose steppe of twilight beaten extremes
began lifting oil lifting despair a deepest forsaken space
wholly liquefied in medley of extremes

Watery Prowler

full folded solar distance fathers forth a kiss a cove a
caulk some canker of thorn soft stars sunk in standing
water the spine of noon broken who have no place inside
me suffer no sense like love to call close some eternity
proposed in description looms or shrinks a simple sway
of trees to say standing across from myself in speech if
I am silent long enough the world pushes through my
face as argument with dead solar distance called close
fugitive targets here a mirror or halo mistaken for solar
source some coin pointing toward a universe civilized
by wealth without return like love dimly aware naming
proposes to call close a symbol as trees standing across
from the world a kind of naming the watery prowler
called beauty between us this argument with the dead
inside language too many voices to explain the world
is silence mistaken for some eternity proposed in
description like love some canker of soft thorn a clock
of stars targeting distance

That Morning We Put Away Anger

brook & babbled brick most ordinary pleasure here &
elsewhere most ordinary hand folding its own weight
we put away back of a face a pause from clear sunday
to junk thursday music of glass folding under that
morning we put away anger as weight of love & table
all depths compounded more & more not elsewhere or
clear sunday pause & most ordinary moonrise nudged
upward the table or a face most ordinary under its own
weight not here & yet not elsewhere giving pleasure
to tend a place from sunday to junk moonrise not the
astonishment capable of most ordinary place the back
of something not here & yet here capable of pleasure or
pause most ordinary that morning we put away anger

Radio Waves Goodbye

highway radio scattering the body we come belated to
my scattering against you through frequencies an alien
opalescent moon fading slow in radio waves goodbye
dummies dropped from government planes come
belated as distance twisted back to prairie through a
mirror radio driving through frequencies fading slow in
mirror distance a place glad to be so lost as if turning
somewhere back in time scattering glad hand in a
mirror waves goodbye everything goodbye scattering
like waves from farmland to prairie to desert voices
through alien frequencies fading to say we come belated
to ourselves

An Invitation to Remain

through a squint thread of light possession dispersed
up & down the river into the center as reaching & wind
brushed flowers her arms empty in morning moon slow
bent by sad snow hyphen inside memory possession
incites gathering to remember gathering to remain the
occasion of her lover up & down the river an invitation
to curve into the snow bent center dispersed under sad
squint thread of light & handful of desert dispersed
when closed a curve gathering empty under snow up &
down the river his limbs dismembered in slow morning
gathering as an invitation to remain

Coda

crickets little spoons
& flag or flock's sequence of time
kinds of grammar

tugged blue troll
net grit & gills

orange blossoms
jerked sprays

plumes of bombs
& jet exhaust

tortoise shell & catgut garden luster
spread like water over a table of air

fists fold to sparrows following
an argument of bread & hunger

the train arrives empty as a house is to caring
confuses self as place
empty as a state of grace

birds move through his head as if a body could enter
the consequence of its own image

past sagged bunting
past sad anthems of lintel sill & glass
a sluggish fugue of trees

so origin has a hand in twists of incident
& disorder's exceeding

the boom swung out too far

man drowned down
under the log jam

beauty's circumference is terror
minding radar's aftermath
& color coded hysterias
gesturing toward fear's transparency

wheat for bolts of silk for example a coat
meaning 10 yards of linen
sheets of beaten clouds push piled light
pressed flat against the air

a coin's congealed labor
lights the universe

siren's aftermath of trash heap's crashed
expenditures persist between
earth's excrement
& unintelligible starlight

so to call close as attention to fugitive targets
like fathers built of silence
who loom or cower
who mean to say
the world is just this violence
the world is just this silence
so to speak's departure
from the dumbbell chime
& unmoved moving crime

light may be speed or music of glass
gathering as to tend the hand
hurt into itself
crushed under the engine block
mangled in the turbine

for those who have neither life nor death
neither vanity nor face
absence proposes place

some depth like a table's pause
between any two
whose place clears away suspension

moon floats in the sidewalk suburban
sprinklers & city lights
shrunk to a mirror's rear view
radio waves goodbye dummies
dropped from government
planes keep our eyes on the sky
as from a distance everything alien
like radio waves fuzzed out behind mesas

Columbine: Robert Duncan, "Santa Cruz Propositions" & "Man's Fulfillment in Order & Strife." Quotes from students, gunmen, mass media, & US Congress regarding the Columbine shootings. Various historical accounts of Columbine, Harlequin, & other *dramatis personae* of Italian comedy.

Evidence: Passages from *The Report of the Chilean National Commission on Truth and Reconciliation.*

Camouflage: Quotes from Pentagon officials regarding cluster bombs & civilian casualties; doctor discussing psychological damage to children injured by picking up unexploded cluster bomb canisters.

Kosovar Child's Still Life with Agitprop: Quotes from ethnic Albanian children in refugee camps; war briefs from NATO & Serbian officials.

Bodies from Rwanda: Donatella Lorch's *New York Times* article, "Bodies from Rwanda Cast a Pall On Lakeside Villages in Uganda" (Kasensero, Uganda, 27 May 1994); entry on "Torture" in Barbara Walker's *The Woman's Encyclopedia of Myths and Secrets.*

Threat Conditions: Homeland Security Advisory System.

CIA Lexicon: From a 41-word English-Arabic lexicon issued to US soldiers in the field.

Democracies of Perception: These pieces evolved out of an interest in the politics of aesthetic form. If language "matters," is there a link between the particle drift of so-called experimental forms & free-market capitalism? the master narrative & big government? What would a democratic syntax look like? how would it differ from the sham democracies of ochlocracy's "here comes everybody" and capitalism's credit card ballot? The first eight sections are comprised of notebook passages fed into the egalitarian dream/nightmare of an online cut-up machine. These pieces were then recombined into individual sections. "Coda" is a lyrical response to the previous pieces.